INSPIRATIONAL POEMS from the HEART

Robert Daniel Malcolm

ISBN 978-1-63630-255-3 (Paperback)
ISBN 978-1-63630-256-0 (Digital)

Covenant Books, Inc.
11661 Hwy 707
Murrells Inlet, SC 29576
www.covenantbooks.com

I met Robert at our community pool one day. It was just him and me alone at this great pool. He introduced himself to me with an ear-to-ear smile. Bob has one arm and a beautiful face. Almost fictional in his disposition, we would talk and get to know each other day by day, not knowing at all about his faith or his writing.

I came to find out that Robert had been writing poems, thoughts, and just inspirational things that came to his head. He has helped me find the Lord and be a better person every day. We have dinner together a lot. He brings his Bible and speaks the word that he thinks would help me through the day. It always works. Please enjoy Robert's works and let him guide you to be you. I want to thank my good friend Robert for all the inspiration and peace in my life.

Your friend,
Michael Przychowicz

My Name Is Bob

I'm a bit of a slob,
But at least I am not a blob.
I like to sing and dance
And make romance with my missy
And swim in pools and seas.
I have three kids
Named Katie, Johnny, and Mary;
And six grandkids
Named Heavyn, Noah, and Hadley
Maxfield, Harlow, and Oliver.
I like to make rhymes and couplets,
And I am so glad I can write
To curb my appetite.
I love to pray.
I find there's no better way
To soothe my soul.
It's even better than rock and roll.
So please remember me
In your prayers if you will,
And I'll remember
You!

Little Blessings Today

Thank you for little blessings today,
Like finding my keys or encouraging
Someone on the narrow way.
Little blessings like air and water
Become big blessings if we have to stay.
And what about laughter and smiles
That help us go extra miles?
Little blessings like that,
Song and flight
That mark the way.
How about unanswered prayer
That calms our nerves?
And here's that help to those.
Why not give blessings today
To carry their load along the way?

The Virus Paradox

Oh no, it's everywhere!
In the news and in your face.
Go away, you stinkin' virus!
Let us resume our lives again.
But thank God something good
Coming out of something bad,
Like counting our blessings,
What we have and hold.

O Lord, Give Us Hope!

O Lord, give us hope when all seems lost,
And You Yourself have paid the cost.
Remember us when it seems to be
No end in sight, except eternity.
Spring forth like a flower,
Looking pretty and nice,
And may we
Remember You paid the price
For our salvation.

Come on in, God

Come on in, God, in the midst of the war.
Protect us and be with us
When we go to work
At the store.
May You be near when I'm in the fire
And bring us out without any sign.
Be with us, God, when the waters
Are deep
And hold us as we swim for safety
So we can keep
Your love.

Alone with God

Oh, how good it is to be alone with God,
And thanks to Him, He spares His rod.
Why not pray
Like there's no other day?
Or sing like a cardinal
And get a beautiful eyeful
Of His wonderful creation?
Why not read His Word
That was written for us?
Or pray to Him
Without any fuss?
Why not watch a movie
Or listen to "Delilah"?
When I do all these things,
I shout,
"Hallelujah!"

At the Pool with Christina

Oh, how I love to meet Christina at the pool.
It's really cool when we're at the pool.
She's so warm and friendly,
Cuddly and nice.
She's a girly girl made of sugar
And spice.
I love when she looks at me
And gives me the eye,
For I know she is happy
When I try.
Oh, I never ever want to make her cry.
My queen, she will forever be,
And I'll never be lonely
With her loving me.

Good News

Don't you love good news,
Which is far better than feeling the blues?
Isn't it great to get a blessing?
And isn't it nice to be caressing?
We can spread good news to you and me,
Saying "Howdy-do" and "How are you?"
As far as the eye can see.
Love one another, have faith and hope,
And remember to pray for the pope.
Come on, get up and bless someone,
And soon you'll be spreading good news
To nearly everyone.

The Pool

Oh, how cool is the pool
When you are hot and sweaty?
Come on, get yourselves ready
For some fun at the pool.
You can swim laps, float in a tube,
Or get yourself tanned.
Come on, man, avoid the sand
And join the band at the pool!

Being Nice

Being nice doesn't cost a dime,
And it makes you feel more sublime.
Being nice is really easy to do.
A smile, a handshake, a "howdy-do"
Will suffice.
It feels good to be nice,
So don't think twice
About being nice.

Why Not Smile?

Why not smile when you walk that extra mile?
If it's not your style to smile,
Just try to see God in everything—
In friends, children playing, trees swaying,
Or snow spraying you as you get wet.
Come on, my friend, please smile.
It's your best bet.

To Swim

Oh, how I like to honor Him
When I swim.
Whether it's sunny and warm,
Or cloudy and cool,
I love to swim in God's swimming pool.
You may wonder why I love to swim so much,
But it makes me feel good
And such and such.

Swimming Is Fun

Swimming is fun, and it is cool
To be sliding along in the ocean or pool.
Isn't it refreshing too
To be cooled off in the summer stew?
Swimming is fun and good exercise.
It's the best form of fitness
We can do.
So come on, let me swim with you.

We Need a Miracle Today

Have you ever heard someone say,
"We need a miracle today?"
Whether it's to save a soul
Or back or arm
To make one whole?
O Lord, you hold the key,
So please listen to our plea
And grant our miracle today.
This week, in Jesus's name,
Who is the same?
Miracle giver
Yesterday, today, and tomorrow.

Rascal, My Friend

Rascal is my friend through and through.
You could never find a more faithful
Friend who is ever so true.
He hangs with his buddy, Snowy the Cat,
And she is much cooler than the Cat in the Hat.
Rascal is funny on the things that he does.
He wrestles his toys until they're almost like fuzz.
And there never will be,
Nor there ever was
Quite a friend like Rascal the Dog.

Where Is Love?

Where is love?
Is it hiding up above?
Unhappy frowns,
Not like clowns
Prevail upon the world.
What is so bad about living?
It is because we forget to be forgiving.
Love is not that far from us.
We just have to seek it.
Only we have the key
To open the door
For more
LOVE.

Christina's the Girl for Me

Oh, can't you see
Christina's the girl for me?
She lights up my day like the sunshine,
And her face is fairer than moonshine.
Christina, Christina, lovely is your body too.
It sends me to the moon and past Timbuktu.
Oh, how I love you,
Christina, my love.

Cooking Is Fun

Cooking is fun whether you cook
For a hundred
Or for one,
Especially when you cook for
That special someone.
What a delight it is to make your
Favorite dish,
Whether it's salad, meat, breakfast, or fish.
Cooking is fun; it's not hard to do.
Be creative; have fun. It's part of you!

Working at McDonald's

Working at McDonald's is fun, you know.
There is no other place I'd like to sow
The seeds of joy to people I know.
We open at five o'clock
When we're barely alive.
There's cooking to do,
More muffins and bagels galore,
And there's cookies and goodies
And biscuits to bake, just to name a few.
And the managers will always
Find you something to do.
One thing I like to do is to cook
On the grill and the dishes too
And saying, "Howdy-do," in the lobby too.
Working at McDonald's is a great job
That can stretch you to the limit,
And that's why I've been there
Twelve years 'cause *I'm lovin' it*.

Go, Phillies, Go

Go, Phillies, Go!
Win the race.
Let's win this year.
Make no mistake
That this year
Should be a piece of cake!
With Doc and Cole,
We can rock and roll.
"O Come, O Come, C. Manual,
Don't disappoint us!"
This we yell.
We love our Phillies! Yes, we do!
"Don't disappoint us through and through!"
This we yell.
We know you can do it! It's not hard to tell!
So come on, Phils, do your best
And lift our spirits
On this glorious quest.

Mr. Fly

Oh, Mr. Fly, I wonder why
You bother me and make me cry.
I don't want to hurt you, so please go away
And come again some other day.
But only for a while,
And then I'll walk a country mile
And see you smile.

Life and Baseball

Life is like baseball,
Sometimes you win; sometimes you lose,
And don't forget to put on the right shoes.
Don your uniform and wear it proudly,
And laugh at yourself and be happy.
Get up to bat and keep on sluggin'
And watch you don't get hit in the noggin'.
Running your bases and you will find
An underlying peace of mind.
Home runs are there for you to do.
Set the score right, and you will love it too.

The Announcer (Harry Kalas)

He announced most every ball game
Until the end,
And one wonders what waits
For him around the bend.
It was so good to hear,
"That ball's outa here!"
When our favorite batter was up.
After all, who doesn't want to
Drink from the cup
Of salvation?
Play by play, he would call them as he saw them,
And isn't that really where it's at?
We're just wild about you, Harry,
You'll be missed, but you left a legacy.

Let's Play Ball

Let's play ball and play the game.
You may end up in the Hall of Fame.
Get up to bat, and you may find
A homer, a triple, or base on balls
Of another kind.
Take your gal or your pal,
There's lots to do, that's for sure.
Buy a hot dog and a beer,
Then sit yourself down and really cheer
For the home team or visitors.
What does it matter?
Only that you play the game,
Whether spectator, infielder, pitcher, or batter.

What Do You Need?

What do you need? Is it food or beer?
Or how about kind words of cheer?
What do you need? Is it money or love?
Why not try praying to your God above?
"Love your neighbor" and "Pick up your cross"
Are certainly better than carrying dross.
What do you need? Is it people or pets?
Or how about forgiving your debts?
What do you need? Will you settle for less
In a small space as a new address,
Where less is more and the basics are plentiful
And giving is better than a barn?
That is plentiful.

Oh, the Dough

Oh no! There is no dough.
No bread, no toilet paper, no food to eat.
This is no trick or treat.
The dough's run out, and what to do?
It's time to get moving through and through.
Sell that stuff, work your job,
Don't lie around like a lazy blob.
Find something to do,
And you may find
The dough will return
And give you peace of mind.

Are You Tired and Weary?

Are you tired and weary and
Have no time to rest?
Don't fret, my friend, you may
Be put to the test.
Work hard, persevere,
Be patient to the rest,
And most of all, when doing your test,
Do your very best.
Don't dwell on how many minutes more
To finish what you do,
But instead, let love empower you.
Don't shove or push where you
Do not belong,
Instead, do right to those
Who have suffered much wrong.
Be patient with yourself and
Friends and persevere really hard,
And you will find much joy
Outside that doesn't fade away.
The blessings you receive
Tomorrow
May be from your work today.

I'm a Pro-Lifer

I'm a pro-lifer; I'm not ashamed to say
That I love life each and every day.
Whether good days or bad,
Happy or sad,
I have to remember
That breath of life sure makes me glad.
The children of mine are so precious to me.
I can't wonder what life would be like
Without my family tree.

Don't Give Up

Keep it up; don't give up.
Laugh it up, and drink your cup.
Love it; don't leave it.
Push, push—don't you shove,
Don't give up; just fall in love.

Why Worry?

Why worry and be in a hurry
When most of what we worry
Never happens?
So don't you fret
Or have regret
Since most of our worry
Is in VAIN.

Day by Day

Live day by day, and you may find
An underlying peace of mind,
Wise and of a kind.
Don't be blind.
You don't know what tomorrow brings,
So sing your song
And don't do wrong.
Be good to others,
And let's love our neighbors
And love your life
Day by day.

When We Pray

When we pray, I often wonder why
Our prayers go to heaven, beyond the sky,
And that God must have an awesome ear
To hear prayers each and every year.
How does He decide what's best for us?
It's hard to know
Whether the answer is yes, just wait,
Or maybe no.
And do we pray with grateful hearts,
Carry our crosses, and play our parts?
Do we try our best each and every day
As God tries to show us the narrow way?

Wake Up

It's time to wake up and say, "Good morning, God,"
And isn't it great to get the nod
And to greet the morn with joy?
And let's face it, it's time to be a man, not a boy.
Look in the mirror, we're made in God's image.
Do you have that beautiful smile
To walk that extra mile?
Wake up and be alive with glee
Because God loves
Both you and me.

The Poetry Man

I'm the poetry man who likes to make you feel
Alive again so you know you are real.
What treasures lie among the word and pen,
It sure beats TV that imprisons you in the den.
My words, I hope, may lift
You up to see a brighter day,
And you may find a ray for you
That's like the sunshine ray.
Poetry man, Poetry man,
Write another verse.
You may be a blessing
Instead of a curse.
Shower your love words on us
And help us live again,
And then we can say we feel good,
And then we don't have to sin.

In the Wilderness

In the wilderness, you may find
A bizarre kind of peace of mind.
No distractions, or coming attractions to you,
But only quiet and solitude, and a sky of blue
Is there waiting for you.
Climb onto new heights or
Descend into valleys below,
Since in the wilderness, there is always snow,
Eagles, hawks, coyotes, and bears,
And we can't forget that really clean air.
So come out of your dwelling
And do some yelling
In the wilderness.

What Is Jesus Like to Me

Jesus is like an every man
With an outstanding tan
Who ran such an outstanding race
That he will never be defeated
Or has never cheated anybody.
His love is deep inside us,
For us to uncover
And discover
That we are His.
And we can talk to Him
And write poems to Him
And praise Him
Because He is so good.
Jesus is the universal body,
Full of great ears, eyes, hands,
Neck, arms, back, and a genius mind.
I don't know how He took the pain
Of the sins of the world,
But I love Him, respect Him, and
I am in awe of Him for doing that.
Thank you, Jesus.

The Awesomeness of Aspen

Aspen is awesome as you may know.
Lots to do and plenty of snow.
Hot tubs galore and outdoor pools
At very high temperatures for woozy fools.
Ski Snowmass, Highlands, or Ajax,
Just have a ball and just relax.
There is a glow
At the valley below.
So come on, let's hurry
And don't you worry,
We'll have an awesome time
At Aspen.

Swoosh, Swoosh, Schuss, Schuss

Swoosh, swoosh, schuss
Went my skis below.
Faster, faster, riding that snow.
As I schuss down the mountain,
Passing people and trees,
Rocketing along with so much ease,
The thrill of adrenaline makes me feel free
As I schuss across the frozen line.

My Pain in the Neck

I have a pain in the neck
That sometimes feels like heck.
It could be worse, you see,
I could be in worse misery.
It is a nuisance,
I'm sure you know
When you've had your
Certain blow.
It's a reminder to me
How Jesus suffered on that tree,
And not just for me,
But for you too.

My Second Chance

Thank you, God, for my second chance,
And I am so glad that I can dance.
Thank you, God, for your mercy on me.
I am so glad you heard my plea.
For a second chance,
I am grateful for this life you gave me,
And may I live each day happily,
Knowing that you love me.
Thank you, God.

To Ski or Not to Ski?
That Is the Question

To ski or not to ski? That is the question.
When I ski, it feels like a part of heaven.
I miss it so much; am I too old
To ski the bumps, to be real bold
Like I used to as I schussed those slopes
And avoided at all costs the
Uncontrollable dopes?
Oh, what fun it is to ski really fast.
What a thrill it was as I skied past
That instructor or bunny queen,
To rush down the hill
Without a spill,
If you know what I mean.
It's so expensive now, I can hardly afford it.
The gear, the condo, is a money pit.
To ski or not to ski?
Only we can decide.

The Air that I Breathe

The air I breathe is a gift.
It can also give you a lift.
When you're feeling low or ill,
It is one of the best blessings we have.
Whether moving or still,
When we're anxious or in a frenzy,
We can take a deep breath, and it will help our tizzy
And, most of all, may help
When we feel dizzy.

The Wolf

Oh, how we're afraid of the big bad wolf!
But, my friend, he's just as afraid
Of you as you are of him
When you meet the big bad wolf.

The Politician

"Howdy-do. How are you?"
Says the politician.
Isn't it great
Of these fifty states
We have so much representation?
Don't forget the good they do
Besides saying "Howdy-do,"
Like helping the poor
Who may have no more
Food or clothing.
It must not be easy
Being very busy
For so many people
And trying to please so many.
So my hat's off to these people
Who have given their lives
To better mankind.

The Next Twenty Years

In the next twenty years, I pray I see
The world's a better place for
You and me.
I pray God's mercy is
Lavished on us
And that we are always on the right bus
And that we don't make a fuss
Over the small stuff.

Hard Times

Hard times come, and hard times go.
Believe it or not, and watch you grow.
Look at that old depression
Who, to a devastating last impression,
It was for some of us.
But that there was the postwar boom,
Unemployment low and hard times few.
Some of us seem to have hard times
More often than others.
Be not afraid, my sisters and brothers,
The Lord is in charge, and He makes our day
For those who seek the narrow way.
Knock and the door may open,
Ask, and it shall be given.
Trust in God and believe,
And the hard times will be only a MEMORY.

The Blahs

Do you have the blahs and feel
Kind of woozy?
Why don't you pray to God to take
Away that feeling?
And He might just set you straight
With another kind of doozy.
Give it to them, that tiredness and blahs today,
And He will get your back on that
Narrow way.
He died so that you and I have an example to be followed,
And it doesn't matter how big that
Sinful pill you swallowed.
That if you ask for forgiveness
And change your way,
He will give you better days.

Journeys

Take me here, take me there,
Take me somewhere I haven't been.
So long as it's not too hot or too cold,
But take me on a journey for the bold.
It could be work, it could be play,
I don't care anyway.
I just need some time to be challenged,
Whether I'm skiing, swimming, or taking
It to the max.
And by the way, I don't like to pay the toll
Someone imposes
When you don't get roses.
Tropic Isles or Sunny Slopes,
Even if we don't elope,
Take me on a journey.

Around the Bend

What treasures wait for you
Around the bend?
With much love and grace for
You to rend?
Don't fret right now because
You are weary.
Around the bend is another story
Where you may find just what you need,
Whether it's joy, love, or food you need.
The road is long, that's for sure,
But you may find your cure
Around the bend.

Don't Get So Down

Don't get so down,
All you do is frown,
And your favorite color is brown.
Find your gift.
Do you catch my drift
To avoid the rift
Between you and others?
So if you had your druthers,
Wouldn't you rather be up
And not be like a sick pup?
Come on, get happy.
You're a good old pappy,
With more miles
Of smiles
For life's journey.

Ask for Help

Ask for help if you need it.
Don't be afraid to share
Your emotions.
We're all in this together
In locomotion.
Talk to a friend, your doctor,
Or family member.
Don't keep it in anymore
So you can render
Peace of mind. (It's there for the asking.)

The Cup

Is your cup empty or full?
Count your blessings to lift you up,
Then you'll be thankful for that half-filled cup.
Drink that cup and realize
Christ died for you to win that prize,
Which is He
Who lives inside of you.
And through that cup, He blesses you.
When you feel low and your cup is empty,
Ask the Lord to fill it up,
And He will and lift you up.

Let's Give Praise

Let's give praise to our God on high,
And how he makes us laugh and cry.
Let's give praise to the Lord above,
Who is filled with precious love.
He's so good; it's plain to see
That He really loves us, you and me.
Just think how He made that sacrifice
For His Son to die to pay the price
For our sins, which are so bad.
But as far as the east is from the west,
He can make us glad.
We are His! Thanks, God.

At the End of the Day

At the end of the day, do you find
You have attained some peace of mind?
Have you touched someone's
Heart and soothed their soul?
Or are you just ready to rock and roll?
And have you gotten yourselves
Ready for tomorrow's run?
And can you look in mirror
And say,
"This day, I found my way,
And I thank God and pray
For another day?"

Pure and Simple

Are your thoughts pure and your actions simple?
You don't need another pimple
That you may get if you stray,
So set yourself on the narrow way.

Good Thoughts

Good thoughts and what we're taught
Are wonderful lessons that can't be bought.
A "Howdy-do" and "How are you?"
Are almost as good as an "I love you."
Let the positive thoughts flow free
In air, over land, and sea.
Remember the good, embrace your love
That was sent to you from above.
And ride out your days
On a wing and a prayer,
And let God take you where
He wants you to be,
Thinking good thoughts
For you and me.

Is it Hot?

"Hot, hot," you say today.
"It's too hot to work.
It's too hot to play,"
You say.
If you try to slow it down,
You may turn the world upside down.
You may be able to do that job
If you don't lie around like a lazy blob.
And you may be able to swim or play,
Because even on a hot day,
Let love find its way
To you today.

We're Spoiled Brats

We're spoiled brats
Who sometimes live like rats,
Competing for food and drink,
And yes, we only think
Of ourselves.
I really dare
To find one who can care
For you.
If you find even one who cares
In some instance, it's really rare.
Why are we chasing the dollar
Which only makes us holler
For more, more?
It's not enough
Because we are spoiled brats.

Time

Rush, rush, hurry, scurry,
I am feeling like Fred MacMurray.
Lots to do, no time to do it,
But please make me not a tuit.
Little by little,
Bit by bit,
Time will help you do it,
Whatever it is you won't go after.
And take the time to plan
For the hereafter.

The Bully

The bully loves to push and shove
His way around; he doesn't love.
He thinks he is so tough and smart
Until his crime is caught
And he realizes
His bullying was all for naught.
Why not be gentle and kind,
Which is easier on one's mind,
Than to charge around
With a mean old frown?

"Work Hard," You Say

"Work hard," you say,
To enjoy today.
Six days you labor,
And once you rest,
Do your best,
And let God take care of the rest.

A Penny Saved

A penny saved is a penny earned.
When you get that money, don't
Let it burn
A hole in your pocket.
You might want to ride on a rocket
Someday for a vacation,
Or your little penny could
Help save someone from starvation.
Save your pennies, and you
Will find
An underlying
Peace of mind.
When you give your pennies to the poor,
It may even be a cure.

Oh, Rain

Oh, rain,
Sometimes you're a pain.
You get in the way and wet my mane.
Oh, rain, you're a blessing and a curse,
And yes, you hurt our purse
When we can't work
Or see a game.
And yet we need you, rain, to make
The crops and flowers grow.
But sometimes, you come down so hard,
It's an awful blow.
Your gray skies aren't as pretty as the blue,
But who am I to say, because,
Rain and clouds, we need you too.

Try Not to Complain

Try not to complain.
Instead, make your sunny lane.
With God, you can make it.
Don't think you can't.
What good does it do to rant
And rave?
You may cause a tidal wave.
So look on the bright side and
Be thankful;
It may help your tank to be full.

Don't Make a Mountain Out of That Molehill

Don't make a mountain out of that molehill.
Enjoy the day,
Whether work or play,
And you will find
The molehill easy to climb.
So don't be your own worst enemy,
But conquer that molehill
And avoid misery.

Rubber Bands, Paper Clips, and Band-Aids

(A Poem for Joan Mary Bromage Poling Malcolm, My Mother)

Look for a rubber band today
To remind you of the narrow way.
How it stretches us to the limit,
But how it snaps back like us to make it.
Find a paper clip to keep it together
To remind us we are held together.
Use a Band-Aid and not forget
The hurt someone got instead of you.
These little reminders help let us see
There is a way for you and me.
Thank you, Mom.

A Tankful of Thankful

How is your tank? Is it half full?
Or at least one-quarter to go forth?
For what it's worth,
I am so thankful for God and Jesus above,
And for His endless love
For you and me
And the blessed trinity.
Thank you for my blessings,
My children, my girlfriend, and my job,
The many graces you've given to Bob (me).
I thank you that I am a sinner
Saved by grace,
And you can take me with you
To that place
Where our tanks are full
And we give thanks
For each moment we have together
With you God, Jesus, Holy Spirit, Mary
And all the saints, families, and friends
Forever.

Love

Love is fleeting; love is blind.
What kind of love do you want?
Or do you want one who will haunt?
Why not spread your ray of sunshine
To others?
Isn't that your real druthers?
Or do you want a significant other?

Peace

Thank you for peace, my God.
There's nothing like getting the nod
From God.
And thank God for your beautiful bod.
Thank you for the air we breathe,
And don't ever leave but cleave to us.

A Night (or Day) with Elvis

The King is gone but not for long.
His music lives on and on.
And let's not forget "Return to Sender"
Is sung by young and old alike,
Whether they're silver-haired or a little tyke.
There's plenty of room for Elvis,
So won't you let me serenade you
Like the King?
Who was *it* and everything
That most everybody likes to sing?

Party Time

It's party time, whether day or night,
And it's the time to set things right.
Forgive and forget, and maybe
Say you're sorry,
So you don't have to worry,
And
You can have a good time at
The party.

Rays of Sun

On a sunny day,
Rays of sun are so much fun.
They make me come undone.
Rays of sun are so fine.
They dwell on my skin,
Like a taste of wine.
Rays of sun sprinkle joy and laughter,
And I think a little glimpse of the hereafter.
Rays of sun sure make me smile
And help me walk that extra mile.
Rays of sun are so special to me,
To be lavished on our family tree.

A Beautiful Day

I pray for a beautiful day;
Oh my god, there's no other way.
Try to get out there and make your way,
And don't forget to clean your tray
To make it through another day.

Clouds

Clouds, clouds, go away,
Come again some other day.
Thank you for the sun so warm,
But without the clouds, there would be no norm.

My Pen

My pen is my friend, you see.
It's given me freedom to be me.
My pen takes me to lofty heights,
And my pen curbs my appetite.
My pen can take me to places unknown,
And my pen can make me groan
With opportunities I have blown.
My pen gives me my success,
And my pen can remind me of my sweet caress
With my sweetheart.
Oh, how I love my pen.
It helps me when
I can't sleep,
To pacify
My anxiousness.
And yes,
Oh, how precious
Is
My pen.

Fences

Fence me in or fence me out,
There is no reason to pout.
Fences are there to keep you out.
Cut these fences and be free,
And you'll be like a honeybee.

Friends

Friends are fun, the friends you've won,
They don't care about your faults,
And they will do somersaults for you.
Friends are groovy. Friends are cool,
And you can find some at the swimming pool.
Friends will love you no matter what,
Whether you're a spot or wrinkle
Or in a rut.
So call a friend, invite them over,
And you will find
Love like no other.

Peace and Quiet

Isn't it nice to get peace and quiet
As opposed to a lot of noise or a riot?
And time to build the bridge of love
For our mind and hearts
Is our Father from up above.
We can lay our burdens down and rest
Because God will help us pass the test.
Do not fret, please cry no more
Because wait until you see
What's in store
Around the bend
For you to rend
From your heavenly Father.

Peace and Love

I wish us peace and love, my dear,
For another year,
And many blessings to you filled with cheer.
Isn't God great to give us peace and love,
And it was sent to us from His undying love?
Isn't it great to love your creator so,
How He lifts us up when we feel low?
The time is now for peace and love,
Which can only be sent from up
Above.

Whine, Whine, and Wine

Oh no, it's your time to whine.
You say, "I can't take it anymore.
I'm out of line."
Why not save your whine for another time?
Remember that He
Is the real wine that you need.

When I Dance

When I dance, I feel so free,
Especially when you're loving me.
I like to sway my arms and legs with ease,
And I like to hold you, if you please.
When I dance, I feel in tune
With the melody,
And you who are so true.
I love to dance;
It's for me and you.

The Happy Day

The happy day
Will come your way,
And oh, will you want to stay
In this happy day?
On this happy day, you will find
Peace for all mankind,
And love will kiss you
And make you blind
To the problems around you.
There may be rain
That causes pain,
But oh, the sun is so bright
On that happy day.
And love will be strong,
You can't feel wrong
On that happy day.
You may sing,
And you may bring
Your happiness for others
On this happy day.

When on Vacation

When on vacation, you may find
That fun, that rest, that peace of mind,
And you may even close the bar.
It may rain,
And you don't complain
Because you find that treasure
That may cause one pleasure.
Don't you worry about time and place;
Just take your mind out of
That rat race.
I hope your joy finds you complete,
And love and peace, rich and poor
Together meet.

When You're Sick

When you're sick, take your blessing,
Look at it as another dressing.
You may look different,
You may look blue,
You may end up in Timbuktu.
But strive on for wellness,
And you may find
Some peace for you of another kind.

Are You Lonely?

Are you lonely, sad, and blue?
Why not let God comfort you?
Do you feel down and out
And feel everyone has left you to pout?
Don't feel so blue;
God hasn't left you.
He's as close as your shadow.
You see, my friend,
He wants to bless you
Around the bend.
So drive that car or
Walk that walk
That will take you there,
And then you will realize He's everywhere.

You Can Cry on My Shoulder

You can cry on my shoulder,
I'll bury your tears,
And you can wail all you want,
I'll try to dispel your fears.
Don't fret any more, my love,
My friend,
God awaits to bless you
Around the bend.
Then those tears of sorrow
Will be gone tomorrow,
And your joy may be full.

Giving Thanks

Do you give thanks to the Lord above
For another day and for love?
Do you give thanks for taking care of your needs,
And are you good at sowing good seeds?
Do you give thanks for the roof over your head,
Especially when you see the homeless with no bed?
Do you give thanks for another meal
And water to drink
That you don't have to steal?
Do you give thanks for the time to enjoy
That special girl or that special boy?
And do you give thanks for the light
So bright
That calms your nerves and makes you feel right?
Do you give thanks Jesus suffered for you?
And in His footsteps, you'll follow
If you want to be true.

Stretching a Dime

Boy, I know a lady who can
Stretch a dime.
She turns it inside out
And makes the finances work out
Most of the time.
In this area and most others,
She is gifted from above.
And not only this,
She does it with love.
When you bust your bank
And you go broke,
Don't you ask some ordinary bloke,
But ask sweet liberty who knows so well
To stretch that dime and make it swell.
With that dime, it's a start to buy
Your way out of a road to ruin.
You'll be out of the red
And into the black and sure to be a shoo-in.
This is all because of the lady
Who can stretch that dime.

The Plane Ride

On the plane, you may find
That you're not just one of a kind.
There's the guy so loud,
You can't hear the crowd,
Or his pride disturbs your ride.
But like the plane, you rise above,
Especially when next to you is your true love
Sent to you from up above.
You may get tossed to and fro
From high winds that blow,
But your faith causes you to feel
A bit more relaxed and on an even keel.
You may talk or you may squawk,
But the plane ride, let's face it,
Is quicker than the walk.

You Warm My Heart

You warm my heart, oh Holy Spirit,
And you will not depart
So long as we keep the flame alive
By praying, reading your word,
And keeping the faith.
Oh, how your fire inside feels right
As we pray with all our might
For forgiveness
As you ease our burden
And clean our slate.
For that flame, oh, breath of God,
Do it now; don't hesitate.
The fire inside feels so good.
As we eat your bread and drink your wine,
Now we know that you make us fine.

The Dance

Won't you dance with me,
My true love?
Let me lead you and love you
Like no other.

Hope

God bless the pope,
He sends us hope.
Come on, you dope,
You don't have to elope.
The future is yours with God's permission,
And you won't need an intermission.
Don't mope, you clown,
Turn that frown
Upside down.
And let that circle of life
That goes round and round,
And you may have found
That hope that makes you sound.

Trust in God

Trust in God with all your might,
And He will help you fight the good fight.
Trust in God, the battle is His,
He cares for you, and that's how it is.
Trust in God and have great faith.
Wait upon Him; don't hesitate.
Trust in God; it's what He wants us to do,
Especially since He
Loves you!

Change the Lens

O God, please change the lens of what I see.
It's discouraging as can be.
Bad news here, wars over there,
Can we please have some fresh air?
Through the eyes of a child,
It's good to see
How far off the mark we can be.
Then let's not take life so seriously.

When in Church

When in church, what do you do?
We are one body, not just a few.
Are you led to give thanks
For grace you don't deserve
When you've done your pranks?
Do you thank God for His endless love
And realize His Son was sent to die
For us? It's the greatest gift from up above.
Do you look at your family
And give thanks
They've turned out okay
Despite their pranks?
Do you pray for all souls
To make it to heaven
As they pray for you?

Mary

Mary, you are so beautiful; you are
Brighter than the brightest star.
The Mother of God, how blessed are you,
How you've cared for us, tried and true.
I love you for that, that's for sure.
Mary, Mary, may your love endure
Forever and ever more.

We Are More Alike

We are more alike than we think.
There are other colors besides pink.
Most of all, make sure you
Don't stink
And that is not a missing link.
Let your heart be your guide,
And let your head not
Slide into your confusion.
Focus on the big picture,
Which is love
That only comes from up above.
Unity without uniformity,
And the trinity is our litany.

The Light

Oh, how wonderful is the light
That makes us feel less uptight.
You will miss the light
If the power goes out,
So hurry to the light before we shout.

Timing Is Everything

Come with me, Lady of Time,
Let's travel together, making rhyme
Out of this mess that we're in
That can be sublime.
They say, "Where does the time go?
Is it wasting away,
And are we hoping for another day?"
We should give thanks for every month
We have,
Not complaining so much about the
Time that we've lost,
But be thankful we have each other
This time.

Lonesome Blue

Why are you so lonesome blue?
Is it because you haven't had a clue?
Or did you get sprayed with
Bird doo?
Come on, you're closer than any crew.
Be comfortable in your own skin,
And that may make you thin
And run like Rin-Tin-Tin
When you're rid of your sin.

I Like to be Alone with God

I like to be alone with God,
To talk to Him as He spares His rod.
He's a loving God, that's for sure.
His love is so vast,
It will endure.
He promises never to leave
Or forsake us,
Wow, what a blessing!
I like to be alone with God,
To talk to Him like a dad or friend.
And I know one thing for sure:
He'll be there in everything
When my heart and soul
Need mending.
God, thanks for caring.

What Do You Need?

What do you need
To make you heed?
That when you lead,
All eyes are on you?
So be very careful.
To be loyal
Lest you slip
And almost flip
Over.
Faith is believing what you can't see.
So come on, blind man,
Receive your amazing grace
And enter the race
Again.

What's in Your Heart?

What's in your heart?
Have you seen?
Is it red, black, or green?
Are you so blind that you can't see
What unkind words do to me?
Why not try nice words? And
You'll find
How loving I'll be and really kind.
Open the door and let God in,
And you'll have a heart of gold
And not of tin.

To Be Witty

To be witty
With nitty-gritty,
It isn't easy.
For words so nutty,
To make your mind
Like
Silly putty.
So try a little bit
To make your mind like your
Wit.

Oak Trees

Oh, these oak trees so strong
And straight,
Never fall unless it's fate.
They stand so tall, with arms so big,
And yet they grew from a little twig.
Oak tree, oak tree, tell your story
Of days gone by, full of glory.
How bare you are from fall
Through winter,
But soon your leaves
Will unfold like glitter.
The woodman's your friend and foe,
But don't forget he makes his dough
On his care for you.
This you know.

When Doing Dishes

When you do the dishes, you may get kisses
From the missus.
So do them right
So she's not uptight,
And you may find
That you may be
Her favorite honey.
So do those dishes,
Not just for money,
And your reward
Will be
To be her knight not just for a night
For the queen bee.

The Lumberjack

The lumberjack is big and strong,
And he seldom can do no wrong.
His cuts are sure, or he may find
He has been a legend in his time.
This woodsman works hard and long,
And his days are very long.
The trees you'd think were his foe,
And yet he loves them and the dough
They give.

When I Make Music

When I make music, I am happy as can be,
Whether whistling, singing, or playing my harp
For you and me.
I love to make those notes so true
That take us all out of the blue.
I play for God, and I play for you,
I play for someone special
Or just a few.
But oh, it gives me so much joy.
No, it isn't just a toy.
It's fun to make a joyful noise
To play for all you girls and boys.
Whether I woo you with a song of love
Or sing a song for God above,
It's all so special to me
To make my melody.

Love

Love is good; love is God.
Love is sparing of the rod.
Love is merciful, love is there,
And it is found in God's breath
Of fresh air.
Love one another, it is said.
Isn't life better
When being fed by
God's love?

Come on Along and
Sing a New Song

One that's never been done,
And one that you'll know,
Come sing a song and be aglow.
Let's sing a new song to glorify our Lord.
Isn't it better to sing than be bored?
Singing cheer at your voice,
Let's sing with love;
Let's make that choice.

When on Jimmy'

When on Jimmy's planet, you may find
A treasure you've been looking for
Of another kind.
It might be
A treasure for you
Or a treasure for me,
Or maybe you sing on his mic
That is there
As your new song sings out of
Thin air.
Or if you are blessed,
You may hear him play his guitar,
Or you may have your picture taken
So you feel like a star,
Who you really are.
Thank you, Jimmy Mack,
Make sure you're coming back
To Jimmy Presley's Planet.

Laugh It Up

Come on, laugh it up
'Cause it won't last.
It is good to laugh; it soothes your soul,
And it can get you out of the hole.
Laugh it up while you still can;
It'll keep you young and looking good, man.
I think it's better than a ton.
Laugh it up and let it out,
It's really better than a snout.
Laugh it up 'cause we are funny;
Just see yourself, and you're on the money.

Meeting God in the Morning (or PM)

What do you do when you greet our God?
Do you say, "Good morning," and give Him the nod?
Don't you marvel at His glorious bod?
He's inside of us, for us to talk,
And on this, I believe He won't squawk.
At our requests,
When we pray,
Do we ask for another day,
Or do we just play
And don't care what's in store for us?
He loves us and cares, though we may not believe
That He's there for us to achieve
Our burdens and trials,
Not for a while,
But are there for us mile after mile
Forever.

God's Sense of Humor

Oh, how funny God really is.
He made us in a whiz,
And we should glorify His biz
Like no other and not fizz.
We are His clowns; He is our director,
But He is the benefactor.
He loves praise and to do our best,
And boy, can He give a test?
But we all find that He is loving,
That He makes us laugh instead of shoving.
He gives us each other
To encourage, not to smother,
To laugh and be filled,
Not drowned or be spilled.
He gives us prayer to communicate,
And don't be late or hesitate
Or be irate.
When He laughs with you,
Remember He made you,
He loves you,
And His promise to you is good, never to leave you.
Believe and you will receive
His smile.

The Irritant

What irritates you? Come on, let's know.
Is it traffic, your boss, or could it be snow?
It's time to put that irritant aside
And go to a new level that's inside.
Irritant, irritant, go away.
But you find when it's gone
A new irritant has won.
So why not look that irritant straight in the eye
And tell him you don't like his style
And place himself on that pile?

Boss Man

Boss man, boss man, speak your thunder.
You're the boss, so make us wonder.
How you get us to do
Things brand-new
At a new level too?
You're not our foe,
You're a friend in disguise
'Cause sometimes, we get your apple pies.
Thank you, boss man, for the money,
And let's not forget
The honey
Too.

At the Bank

At the bank, do you find
Some kind of peace of mind?
And there's tellers for you who are very kind
At the bank.
You're there for transactions,
And you hope to attain satisfaction
That your account's in the black
And there is no lack
Of funds.
So make that deposit, or
Make that withdrawal.
When you leave the bank,
Are you happy or sad?
As I speak for myself, I am
Mostly glad.

The Teacher

Teacher, teacher, can you reach her?
She's been dormant for so long,
There's no way she can learn
Unless she tries
To start anew
And find what makes her glow.
Is it rewards that you know
That only you can bestow?
I'm a teacher and student,
And we are in life's classroom.
What have you learned?
And what have you taught?

The Best Things in Life Are Free

The best things in life are free.
Don't put a price tag on a smile,
Or on walking that happy mile,
Or the sun beaming on a cloudy day,
Or work you enjoy at the end of the day.
When you laugh and communicate,
And how about reading a license plate?
The best things in life are free; it's
Been known
That when we're in love.
We don't always moan,
But let's face it,
We don't own
The very best things which are
Free:
The gift of life,
A good wife,
And our Jesus,
Who offered His life.
So the best things in life are free.

The Lesson

The lesson's not easy, and yet it's not hard
To repeat the mistake and to not retard
Into doing dumb stuff now and again
Because it really irritates your friend.
Your true friend will tell you what's wrong
So you don't hit your head with a bong.
That's how God gets my attention
When I don't learn my lesson.
Oh, chip on your shoulder better,
Knock it off,
The cost he paid
And the ransom for many
Was a lesson that cost a pretty penny.
Stop your whining and complaining.
Would you rather it stop raining?
Stop your mistakes before it's too late,
And there is no room to hesitate
For a date with fate,
Who may have you for supper.

Aruba

Aruba is not shaped like a tuba.
It's more like a fish
Where you can scuba.
It's eighty-five degrees most of the time.
It rains mostly never
But is sunny forever.
Most of the time,
You can dance,
You can take a big chance
At the table
If you feel you are able.
But isn't it more fun
To play in the sun?
Oh, happy are we
Under the palm tree.
We love Aruba, the sea, and the sky so blue.
I think you might like Aruba too.

The Weather

"Don't let the weather get you down," you say,
But isn't it better to see that sunny day
Than to see clouds and shiver your life away?
Oh, spring and summer, hurry your way.
Please don't tarry,
It's a good time to marry.
Rays of warm sunshine do your stuff
Because this cold's been really tough,
And to tell you the truth,
We've had enough.
"But would you rather live in Alaska
With little warmth and little
Light in winter?"
This I ask you.

Your Kiss

Your kiss I really miss,
And you never miss
With that sweet loving kiss.
When our lips meet,
Tough and tender,
You make me feel like singing
"Return to Sender."
Your kiss is like no other
From all the rest.
You are the best,
You are like no other,
And I don't want another's
Kiss.

Prayer

Oh, how prayer works to the highest degree.
Miracles await you and me.
All you have to do is ask for your need
To the man who suffered and died for you indeed.
Ask Him to help you bear your cross,
And you won't suffer much
Or feel your loss.

I Love to Sing

I love to sing; it makes me happy,
Even though some call me sappy.
I am a happy grandpappy.
There's Christina and my family
That make me sing my melody.
Oh, let me sing, loud and clear,
Even if it hurts your ear.
Listen up, and you may find
You, like I, get peace of mind
When I sing.

Dr. Grink

I have a great doctor named
Corey Grink,
And you know he's like the missing
Link.
He listens and speaks with
Such wisdom, you know,
And he's well versed on almost
Any topic you throw.
He's got a good sense of humor
And is a family man too.
He knows what to do to,
What ails you
Through and through.
So if you ache in your back,
He'll put you on track.
There's little he'll miss,
And he'll help pain go amiss.
So why not give him a try,
This fantastic guy
Dr. Grink?

The Promise

Promise me this and promise me that,
Do you really know where it's at?
Don't be full of baloney and b.s.,
But rather actions and pass the test.
To never say "never" and never say "always"
And deliver what you say
Are the best ways.

Watching TV

I used to hardly watch TV,
And now it's you and me
That watch TV.
The best thing I like about TV
Is it keeps me company,
And I get to see
My favorites on TV.

Keep Going On

Keep going on, although it's late
For fate to hesitate.
Enjoy the pleasures you've been given,
And always give thanks that you're
Forgiven, if you ask God
To forgive the blunders you have made.
Come on, keep going.
Heart's a rowing,
You always get to the other side.
Sing your song,
Dance that dance,
Why not take another chance?
You may stop for a rest.
This is done by all the best.
But pick up that pace
And reenter that race
God gave you.

My Car

My car is better by far
Than a walk in the park.
My car drives like a lark,
And the good thing is, it
Doesn't bark.
My car is as basic as it can be.
My car is a lot like me,
A little buzzing honeybee (Hyundai).
It's good on gas
And has snazzy mats,
And it's good for storing
My McDonald's hats.
My car runs good,
And I can count on it.
I'm so glad I didn't buy
A piece of… (guess).

Christmas Morning

T'was the night before Christmas,
And I was all by myself.
I was feeling like a bad little elf
When my phone died and I had
To put it on a shelf.
And that wasn't all; I was
Also low on gas,
So I decided to move this body
To where it belonged:
In church.
Where I was fed spiritual food
To put me in a good mood.
God bless, Jesus,
For dying for me,
So I discovered what was
Best for me,
To be in God's house,
Worshipping Him
And not me.

My Beard

I like my beard
As you may see.
The whiskers are a lot like me.
My Don Quixote look is sharp,
And you ought to hear me
Play the harp.
My beard is trimmed
Very neat,
And it keeps me warm
When there is no heat.
My beard is liked by others
And me,
And it's not coming off
As you can see.

Counting Your Blessings

Do you feel your life's a mess?
Well, why not think how much
You are blessed?
Don't you fret or cry no more,
Because wait until you see
What's in store.
Inside that old hardened heart
Lies a jolly old fart,
Who's really a lot of laughs.
Come on, stop crying,
Life can be a gas,
So stop being a horse's ass
And get with the program
And start living,
For life's not for the taking
But FOR GIVING.

I Thank God

I thank God for everything,
For my sweetheart and birds that sing.
I thank God for all the joy,
And for what I did when I was a boy.
I thank God for skies so blue
And rain that makes the flowers too.
I thank God for good health,
Which is far better than all the wealth
We could ever own.
I thank God for my little home (apt.),
It's like a slice of heaven
Where I can find
My peace of mind
And be with God
Every morning, noon, and night.
I thank God for my little car,
It really can take me pretty far.
I thank God that I can laugh,
And that God is good
And life is too.

What's Your Story?

What's your story?
Is it full of glory,
Or tales of woe?
How you lost your dough?
What's your story?
Are you a servant?
Or are you being served?
Or are you both?
Who takes out the trash in your house?
It certainly isn't Mickey Mouse.
What's your story?
Are you a lover or fighter?
A day person or an all-nighter?
What's your story? Is your soul alive
With joy for your God
Who'll give you the high five,
Where you make Him number one?

Leaves

I cleave to my leaves, you see.
No, I am not a tree.
But I make money for you and me
From leaves.
Those piles of gold and orange you hate
Will help me pay that bill, not late.
Those cruddy, smelly, slimy leaves
Also help me put food on the table.
I love to rake, and it helps my back
And neck,
Even though you have to rake.
It makes money for heaven's sake.

Going to Mary's

Going to Mary's
Is a happy time.
To see her, Hadley, and Dave,
And what about their new
Addition, Heavyn.
Who is heaven's seat?
When going to Mary's, I hear tales galore.
It's never a bore as we talk and we listen
About our family,
Which really makes my heart happy.
Her home is so neat and clutter-free,
And it's really wonderful to be
At Mary's.

Thank God It's Friday

Thank God it's Friday
And all is well,
And there's no bad news today
For us to tell.
Friday's like one
Big wishing well,
Where dreams come alive
And we're done at work by five.
To eat, to drink, and be merry,
And maybe we'll take the
Cape May Ferry.
As long as we're not in a hurry,
We won't miss the boat,
And my vote
For the best day of the week
Is Friday.

As the Crow Flies

Which way does that crow fly?
And do you hear him squawk
And cry at you
To pay attention to
Him for a moment or two?
They say he has twenty-five words,
Enough to scare off these herds
Of beasts and other birds.
The crow is black and looks
Real mean,
But he's really a comic
Underneath
His dark scary exterior,
And he's really a good
Guy on his interior.
Don't brag too much,
Or you may find
You may go blind
Someday.
Or maybe yet you may
Have to eat that crow.

Sunny Days

Oh, how I love those sunny days
And to catch God's beautiful rays.
The earth's so bright and clean, you'll see,
And there really is beauty in a tree
For you and me.
The grass is so green; the snow is so white,
And I feel less uptight
On those sunny days.
So, sunshine, pour out your
Rays of love
From up above,
And you may see that peaceful dome
On God's sunny days.

The Day After Christmas

Are you relieved
That you truly believed
That the day after Christmas
Isn't a mess
But is still the best time of the year?
You have time to rest
And put those toys and gifts.
You were given to the test,
And then you realize you are
Truly blessed
By a smile or a kiss
Or something you missed
But appreciate now
On the day after Christmas.
God giveth, God taketh,
And God gives back again.
And I would rate yesterday and today
A wonderful ten.

Christmas Cards

Christmas cards are great to get,
And some will get you out of debt.
Christmas cards send love and cheer,
And you can look at them any
Time of the year.
They mean so much to me,
Even more than my little
Christmas tree.
You may receive
The reason to believe
In a Christmas card.

Katie and Jamie

It was so great to hear
From you and Jamie, who bring cheer.
You've both been a gift from above,
And no wonder I love you so much.
We wish you both the very best.
Work really hard but get your rest.
Believe in God and do your best.

What's to Eat?

What's to eat?
Do you have your meat
And potatoes,
Or do you like tomatoes?
What's to eat?
Good food or junk food
To put you in a good mood,
And do you have enough food
To feed your brood,
Or are they hungry as heck?
Well, why not go and risk your neck
And bring home the bacon
On your trek?

Pain

Pain, pain, go away.
Don't come again until some other day.
All of us just keep on complaining,
When will that pain ever start waning?
A pill for this; a pill for that.
Sometimes I feel like a laboratory rat.
When all I need to ease the pain
Is a hug, a kiss, or a little rain,
So get on the love train to
Ease your pain.
Lest you might be in the
Losing lane.

It All Snaps Back

It all snaps back
Like a rubber band,
And what about people who give you a
Hand
And give you something to eat
That would beat
The band?
It all snaps back,
And you will find
Your health, your wealth,
And peace of mind comes back too.
So don't give up, not for a minute,
Because life is great,
Especially when YOU'RE IN IT.

Dreams

Dreams, dreams, dreams
Flow like streams.
Some are rough and some are refreshing,
But some are just an expression
Of our fears and hopes.
And sometimes we feel we're on the ropes
And can't wait for the bell
To wake us up.
Some are good, and some are bad.
Some are happy and some are sad.
But isn't it better to dream
Than not at all?

My Hands

My hands were made by God
Who has given me the nod.
To cook, to clean, to stay lean,
And write another verse,
And this isn't a curse,
And someday could help my purse.
But until that day, I love my time
Making couplets, making rhyme,
And maybe for a while,
I'll make you smile.

My Hands: Part 2

My hands will do the praying.
My hands were made for playing.
My hands were made for writing.
My hands were made for caressing
And also made for dressing.
My hands were made for embracing you
Because I love you.

Smiles

Some smiles are pretty,
And some smiles are handsome.
Some smiles are silly,
And some smiles are flirtatious.
But one thing that's for sure,
A smile is better than a frown,
Which is a smile turned upside down.

She Smells Good

She smells good, like a flower.
And oh, how it makes me shower,
To smell as good as her.
She smells good all the time.
She smells much better
Than any fine wine.
That's because she is so fine.
A queen of hearts
Does not smell tart,
And my queen is what
She is.

The Light

Darkness, darkness, don't dwell in here.
Isn't it a bit like beer?
That darkness
Where that beer lies in the dark keg,
I'd much rather keep my arm and leg.
As the light slowly appears,
It's refreshing and not depressing
To see
The light of day.
Dawn, come out here.
Dark, go away.
To see the light of another day
Is truly a blessing.

Son Light, Sun Bright

Oh, Son light, sun bright, shine your grace
On us.
Take our hands, lead us home,
Especially when we roam.
Sometimes, the world is so hard.
It's hard to get up and not retard.
Sunlight, sunlight, shower us with love.
Guide us and abide in us
And share heaven above.

Step Out

Step out of your hole,
You little troll,
And see what the light of day
Has in store for you.
A blessing or two
For you to discover today.
Go out in this world
And tell the news
To forget all your blues.
For your savior is near,
He is right in here.
Close to your heart
And won't depart.
So keep the faith,
Step out and shout,
"The Lord is coming soon
To straighten out the earth in tune,
And His steps are true."

Morning Time

Aren't you glad you were born in the morn?
Where the sun's so bright
And you feel just right,
To start another day,
To get on your way,
Whether work or play.
The morning is for you.

Shine On

Shine on, dear Son, who is so bright.
Shine on, blaze on with all your might.
You're a friend to us; you keep us warm,
And it's good to see you in the morn.
Shine on, dear sun, and send those rays,
Which really bring us happy days.
Your Son is strong; your Son is loving,
And we like what we're becoming.
Shine on, dear Son, and let us see
All the mercies you've got in there.
Shine on, dear Son, and let us live
Forever with you here
And there.

Dad's Plane

Dad's plane is up in the sky,
For me to be wondering why
He has to fly
Day and night
To watch over me
Like a wayward bee.
It never quits hovering around,
And he usually appears
When he is applauding me
And lauding me,
And then his plane disappears
Until the next time
I do something fine.
Fly on, dear Dad,
Till we meet again
When it's time.

(Dad, Reid Welsh Malcolm, I love you.)

I Love to Sing

I love to sing
About everything.
It's hard for me now,
But someday I'll take that
Gracious bow
When I sing again.

The Bike Rides

The bike rides I take are for
Work and play,
And sometimes, they speed me toward
Another day.
The bike rides I take aren't really long,
And there's a pleasure I get when I sing
My song on my bike.
The wind on my face is really great,
So get on your bike, don't hesitate.

Dress for Success

You must look your best,
Whatever you do,
Whether you're out on a date or at work late.
Polish your shoes, straighten that tie,
And always dress up when you're going to fly.
Starch that shirt and get out that wrinkle,
Clean those glasses so your eyes
Can twinkle.
Comb that hair,
Trim that beard,
And try not to look very weird.
Wear matched socks,
Put on cologne,
You don't want to be alone.
When you dress for success, you may find,
It'll put a smile on you
Of another kind.

Snow

What's that falling out of the sky?
I wonder why as I look really high.
I see flakes shimmering like crystal,
Sharp as a pistol.
To some, this snow is one big pain,
But I would rather see snow than rain,
And this snow that is so cold
Can produce dollars for us like gold.
As we dig our way out, you may see
A neighbor long gone, who's been
A friend to me.
This snow drapes the landscape
With its lovely white,
Which helps us to see in the late night.
So, come on, my friend, don't get uptight
About the snow, which will be gone
And the season of spring
Will be a blow to the snow
And melt it away
Until its ending.

Following My Star

I will follow that star as long as I live,
And that means I must always forgive
The wrongs people do
And their misdeeds too.
I will follow that star that was made for me
As unreachable as it seems to be.
Sometimes, it's so dark when I follow,
And that's a hard pill to swallow.
But when I follow that star, I must
Give my best
Not to be always like the rest,
But strive on for the glorious quest,
And then I will attain my peaceable rest.

I Am Sorry (to God)

I am sorry for I'm a sinner.
No, I'm not a pro or just a beginner,
But just one who needs grace
To keep me running in the race.
I love it that our God is kind
And that He doesn't mind
Our bad mistakes, just as long as we
Don't keep making them our two and three.
He forgives the wrongs we do
Because He loves us both, me and you.

My Walk with God

My walk with God is a pleasure for sure,
And He makes it fun to endure
The hardships and trials we face
By taking us to another place.
There's blue skies to look at up above,
And guys and dolls that are in love.
I see so much I can't explain,
Even when I walk in the rain.
There's vibrant colors of green and blue,
And there is your girlfriend waiting for you
To come home to a warm, cozy home.
So you don't have to moan
And walk too far to catch the phone.
My walk with God includes people too,
And sometimes saying, "Howdy-do."
My walk with God is so much fun that I
Wonder what that walk's like
With Him in the sky.
We'll want to find out, for when it's time
For me to stop work on a dime,
For when He calls me home,
I'll be ready for sure
To enter through that holy door!

About the Author

Robert Daniel is a seventy-year-old (young at heart) man who has been blessed abundantly. He has three children—Katie, Mary, and John—and six grandchildren: Hadley, Heavyn, Harlow, Maxfield, Noah, and Oliver. He loves to write, pray often, and sing in the St. Catherine of Siena choir. He also enjoys traveling. He has been in forty-three states—a mission trip to England, Mexico, the Bahamas, and Jamaica. He is also a cancer survivor, thanks be to God.